Praying Prosperity into My Life

A 13-Week Prayer Devotional Journal

International Award-Winning Author Toneal M. Jackson

www.WeAreAPS.com

Copyright © 2020 by Toneal M. Jackson

All rights reserved.

No portion of this book may be reproduced mechanically, electronically, or by any other means, including photocopying, without written permission of the publisher.

ISBN: 978-1-945145-55-1

Author's Note

The purpose of the Prayer Devotional Journal is to lead you into a lifestyle of prayer by becoming more acquainted with God. Prayer is our way of communicating with God. More than just a moment of providing a list of demands (the things we want and need), prayer is a spiritual state of mind. It is a time where we not only speak *to* God but wait to hear *from* God.

Our prayer lives may lack substance because we don't pray on a consistent basis. Oftentimes, I've heard people say, "I don't know how to pray" or even, "I don't know what to pray." This interactive Prayer Devotional Journal is designed to teach methods of prayer. There is a weekly scripture provided, an explanation as to how the given scripture applies to you, as well as a prayer tip that can help improve your prayer life.

Week 1

3 John 1:2

"Dear friend, I pray that you may enjoy good health and that all may go well with you, even as your soul is getting along well."

Explanation

Live your best life. Understand that true prosperity is more than financial wealth; it is a combination of good physical, mental, spiritual and financial health.

Prayer Tip

Ask God to keep you well-balanced in every aspect of your life.

Monday

How can living a well-balanced life benefit your partner? Take time to communicate to God why you believe this request to be important for your significant other.

My prayer for my spouse (partner):

_____
_____
_____
_____
_____
_____
_____
_____
_____
_____
_____
_____
_____

Tuesday

How can living a well-balanced life benefit your child(ren)? Take time to communicate to God why you believe this request to be important for him/her/them.

My prayer for my child(ren):

_____
_____
_____
_____
_____
_____
_____
_____
_____
_____
_____
_____
_____

Wednesday

How can living a well-balanced life benefit your family? Take time to communicate to God why you believe this request to be important for them.

My prayer for my family:

Thursday

How can living a well-balanced life benefit your church and pastor? Take time to communicate to God why you believe this request to be important for them.

My prayer for my church and pastor:

_____
_____
_____
_____
_____
_____
_____
_____
_____
_____
_____
_____
_____
_____

Friday

How can living a well-balanced life benefit your boss/co-workers? Take time to communicate to God why you believe this request to be important for them.

My prayer for my boss/co-workers:

_____
_____
_____
_____
_____
_____
_____
_____
_____
_____
_____
_____

Saturday

How can living a well-balanced life benefit your enemy? Take time to communicate to God why you believe this request to be important for them.

My prayer for my enemy/enemies:

_____
_____
_____
_____
_____
_____
_____
_____
_____
_____
_____
_____
_____
_____
_____

Sunday

How can living a well-balanced life benefit you? Take time to communicate to God why you believe this request to be important.

My prayer for myself:

_____
_____
_____
_____
_____
_____
_____
_____
_____
_____
_____
_____
_____

Week 2

Deuteronomy 1:11

"May the Lord, the God of your ancestors, increase you a thousand times and bless you as He has promised."

Explanation

You should be happy when others prosper. You should not possess jealousy or envy in your heart, but you should be able to genuinely wish others well.

Prayer Tip

Ask God to take away any feelings of malice, envy or jealousy.

Monday

How can possessing a true sense of joy for others benefit your partner? Take time to communicate to God why you believe this request to be important for your significant other.

My prayer for my spouse (partner):

_____
_____
_____
_____
_____
_____
_____
_____
_____
_____
_____
_____

Tuesday

How can possessing a true sense of joy for others benefit your child(ren)? Take time to communicate to God why you believe this request to be important for him/her/them.

My prayer for my child(ren):

_____
_____
_____
_____
_____
_____
_____
_____
_____
_____
_____
_____
_____

Wednesday

How can possessing a true sense of joy for others benefit your family? Take time to communicate to God why you believe this request to be important for them.

My prayer for my family:

_____
_____
_____
_____
_____
_____
_____
_____
_____
_____
_____
_____
_____

Thursday

How can possessing a true sense of joy for others benefit your church and pastor? Take time to communicate to God why you believe this request to be important for them.

My prayer for my church and pastor:

_____
_____
_____
_____
_____
_____
_____
_____
_____
_____
_____
_____
_____
_____

Friday

How can possessing a true sense of joy for others benefit your boss/co-workers? Take time to communicate to God why you believe this request to be important for them.

My prayer for my boss/co-workers:

_____
_____
_____
_____
_____
_____
_____
_____
_____
_____
_____
_____

Saturday

How can possessing a true sense of joy for others benefit your enemy? Take time to communicate to God why you believe this request to be important for them.

My prayer for my enemy/enemies:

_____
_____
_____
_____
_____
_____
_____
_____
_____
_____
_____
_____
_____

Sunday

How can possessing a true sense of joy for others benefit you? Take time to communicate to God why you believe this request to be important.

My prayer for myself:

_____
_____
_____
_____
_____
_____
_____
_____
_____
_____
_____
_____
_____

__Week 3__

Deuteronomy 1:21

"Look, the Lord your God has set the land before you; go up and possess it, as the Lord God of your fathers has spoken to you."

Explanation

God has already given you what you desire, but you must be willing to do what is necessary to possess it.
You must be willing to obey God.

Prayer Tip

Pray that God removes all doubt and fear.

Monday

How can removing the spirit of fear benefit your partner? Take time to communicate to God why you believe this request to be important for your significant other.

My prayer for my spouse (partner):

Tuesday

How can removing the spirit of fear benefit your child(ren)? Take time to communicate to God why you believe this request to be important for him/her/them.

My prayer for my child(ren):

_____
_____
_____
_____
_____
_____
_____
_____
_____
_____
_____
_____
_____
_____

Wednesday

How can removing the spirit of fear benefit your family? Take time to communicate to God why you believe this request to be important for them.

My prayer for my family:

_____
_____
_____
_____
_____
_____
_____
_____
_____
_____
_____
_____
_____
_____

Thursday

How can removing the spirit of fear benefit your church and pastor? Take time to communicate to God why you believe this request to be important for them.

My prayer for my church and pastor:

_____
_____
_____
_____
_____
_____
_____
_____
_____
_____
_____
_____
_____

Friday

How can removing the spirit of fear benefit your boss/co-workers? Take time to communicate to God why you believe this request to be important for them.

My prayer for my boss/co-workers:

_____
_____
_____
_____
_____
_____
_____
_____
_____
_____
_____
_____

Saturday

How can removing the spirit of fear benefit your enemy? Take time to communicate to God why you believe this request to be important for them.

My prayer for my enemy/enemies:

_____
_____
_____
_____
_____
_____
_____
_____
_____
_____
_____
_____
_____

Sunday

How can removing the spirit of fear benefit you? Take time to communicate to God why you believe this request to be important.

My prayer for myself:

_____
_____
_____
_____
_____
_____
_____
_____
_____
_____
_____
_____

Week 4

Psalms 37:34

"Put your hope in the Lord. Travel steadily along his path. He will honor you by giving you the land. You will see the wicked destroyed."

Explanation

Don't put your trust in anyone but God. When you have faith in Him and obey His voice and His will for your life, He will bless you. Your enemies won't even be a factor.

Prayer Tip

Ask God to increase your faith.

Monday

How can trusting God completely benefit your partner? Take time to communicate to God why you believe this request to be important for your significant other.

My prayer for my spouse (partner):

_____
_____
_____
_____
_____
_____
_____
_____
_____
_____
_____
_____
_____

Tuesday

How can trusting God completely benefit your child(ren)? Take time to communicate to God why you believe this request to be important for him/her/them.

My prayer for my child(ren):

_____
_____
_____
_____
_____
_____
_____
_____
_____
_____
_____
_____
_____

Wednesday

How can trusting God completely benefit your family? Take time to communicate to God why you believe this request to be important for them.

My prayer for my family:

_____
_____
_____
_____
_____
_____
_____
_____
_____
_____
_____
_____
_____

Thursday

How can trusting God completely benefit your church and pastor? Take time to communicate to God why you believe this request to be important for them.

My prayer for my church and pastor:

_____
_____
_____
_____
_____
_____
_____
_____
_____
_____
_____
_____
_____
_____

Friday

How can trusting God completely benefit your boss/co-workers? Take time to communicate to God why you believe this request to be important for them.

My prayer for my boss/co-workers:

_____
_____
_____
_____
_____
_____
_____
_____
_____
_____
_____
_____
_____

Saturday

How can trusting God completely benefit your enemy? Take time to communicate to God why you believe this request to be important for them.

My prayer for my enemy/enemies:

_____
_____
_____
_____
_____
_____
_____
_____
_____
_____
_____
_____
_____
_____

Sunday

How can trusting God completely benefit you? Take time to communicate to God why you believe this request to be important.

My prayer for myself:

_____

_____

_____

_____

_____

_____

_____

_____

_____

_____

_____

_____

Week 5

1 Kings 2:3

"Observe the requirements of the Lord your God and follow all His ways. Keep the decrees, commands so that you will be successful in all you do."

Explanation

True success comes as a result of complete obedience to God. When you walk in your purpose and fulfill His laws, He will ensure that you have all that you need.

Prayer Tip

Pray that God increases your ability to focus.

Monday

How can an increased sense of focus benefit your partner? Take time to communicate to God why you believe this request to be important for your significant other.

My prayer for my spouse (partner):

_____
_____
_____
_____
_____
_____
_____
_____
_____
_____
_____
_____
_____

Tuesday

How can an increased sense of focus benefit your child(ren)? Take time to communicate to God why you believe this request to be important for him/her/them.

My prayer for my child(ren):

_____
_____
_____
_____
_____
_____
_____
_____
_____
_____
_____
_____

Wednesday

How can an increased sense of focus benefit your family? Take time to communicate to God why you believe this request to be important for them.

My prayer for my family:

_____
_____
_____
_____
_____
_____
_____
_____
_____
_____
_____
_____
_____

Thursday

How can an increased sense of focus benefit your church and pastor? Take time to communicate to God why you believe this request to be important for them.

My prayer for my church and pastor:

_____
_____
_____
_____
_____
_____
_____
_____
_____
_____
_____
_____
_____
_____

Friday

How can an increased sense of focus benefit your boss/co-workers? Take time to communicate to God why you believe this request to be important for them.

My prayer for my boss/co-workers:

_____
_____
_____
_____
_____
_____
_____
_____
_____
_____
_____
_____

Saturday

How can an increased sense of focus benefit your enemy? Take time to communicate to God why you believe this request to be important for them.

My prayer for my enemy/enemies:

_____
_____
_____
_____
_____
_____
_____
_____
_____
_____
_____
_____
_____

Sunday

How can an increased sense of focus benefit you? Take time to communicate to God why you believe this request to be important.

My prayer for myself:

_____
_____
_____
_____
_____
_____
_____
_____
_____
_____
_____
_____
_____

Week 6

Joshua 1:8

"Study this Book of Instruction continually. Meditate on it day and night so you will be sure to obey everything written in it. Then you will be prosperous and successful."

Explanation

You must study and obey
the word of God.
Everything you need to know to
succeed in life
is contained therein.

Prayer Tip

Ask God to help you make studying His word a priority.

Monday

How can studying the word of God benefit your partner? Take time to communicate to God why you believe this request to be important for your significant other.

My prayer for my spouse (partner):

_____
_____
_____
_____
_____
_____
_____
_____
_____
_____
_____
_____
_____
_____

Tuesday

How can studying the word of God benefit your child(ren)? Take time to communicate to God why you believe this request to be important for him/her/them.

My prayer for my child(ren):

_____
_____
_____
_____
_____
_____
_____
_____
_____
_____
_____
_____
_____
_____

Wednesday

How can studying the word of God benefit your family? Take time to communicate to God why you believe this request to be important for them.

My prayer for my family:

_____
_____
_____
_____
_____
_____
_____
_____
_____
_____
_____
_____
_____

Thursday

How can studying the word of God benefit your church and pastor? Take time to communicate to God why you believe this request to be important for them.

My prayer for my church and pastor:

_____
_____
_____
_____
_____
_____
_____
_____
_____
_____
_____
_____
_____

Friday

How can studying the word of God benefit your boss/co-workers? Take time to communicate to God why you believe this request to be important for them.

My prayer for my boss/co-workers:

_____
_____
_____
_____
_____
_____
_____
_____
_____
_____
_____
_____
_____

Saturday

How can studying the word of God benefit your enemy? Take time to communicate to God why you believe this request to be important for them.

My prayer for my enemy/enemies:

_____
_____
_____
_____
_____
_____
_____
_____
_____
_____
_____
_____
_____

Sunday

How can studying the word of God benefit you? Take time to communicate to God why you believe this request to be important.

My prayer for myself:

_____
_____
_____
_____
_____
_____
_____
_____
_____
_____
_____
_____
_____

Week 7

Jeremiah 29:11

"For I know the plans I have for you, declares the Lord, plans to prosper you and not to harm you, plans to give you hope and a future."

Explanation

Even when you are uncertain of the purpose for your life, trust that God not only knows, but has plans that are in your best interest.

Prayer Tip

Ask God for the spirit of discernment.

Monday

How can possessing the spirit of discernment benefit your partner? Take time to communicate to God why you believe this request to be important for your significant other.

My prayer for my spouse (partner):

_____
_____
_____
_____
_____
_____
_____
_____
_____
_____
_____
_____
_____

Tuesday

How can possessing the spirit of discernment benefit your child(ren)? Take time to communicate to God why you believe this request to be important for him/her/them.

My prayer for my child(ren):

_____
_____
_____
_____
_____
_____
_____
_____
_____
_____
_____
_____
_____

Wednesday

How can possessing the spirit of discernment benefit your family? Take time to communicate to God why you believe this request to be important for them.

My prayer for my family:

_____
_____
_____
_____
_____
_____
_____
_____
_____
_____
_____
_____
_____
_____

Thursday

How can possessing the spirit of discernment benefit your church and pastor? Take time to communicate to God why you believe this request to be important for them.

My prayer for my church and pastor:

_____
_____
_____
_____
_____
_____
_____
_____
_____
_____
_____

Friday

How can possessing the spirit of discernment benefit your boss/co-workers? Take time to communicate to God why you believe this request to be important for them.

My prayer for my boss/co-workers:

_____
_____
_____
_____
_____
_____
_____
_____
_____
_____
_____

Saturday

How can possessing the spirit of discernment benefit your enemy? Take time to communicate to God why you believe this request to be important for them.

My prayer for my enemy/enemies:

_____
_____
_____
_____
_____
_____
_____
_____
_____
_____
_____
_____
_____
_____

Sunday

How can possessing the spirit of discernment benefit you? Take time to communicate to God why you believe this request to be important.

My prayer for myself:

_____
_____
_____
_____
_____
_____
_____
_____
_____
_____
_____
_____

Week 8

Proverbs 11:25

*"A generous person
will prosper;
whoever refreshes others
will be refreshed."*

Explanation

Be willing to give cheerfully.
You will reap what you sow.
What you do to others
will be done to you.

Prayer Tip

*Pray that God gives you
a giving heart.*

Monday

How can being generous benefit your partner? Take time to communicate to God why you believe this request to be important for your significant other.

My prayer for my spouse (partner):

_____
_____
_____
_____
_____
_____
_____
_____
_____
_____
_____
_____
_____

Tuesday

How can being generous benefit your child(ren)? Take time to communicate to God why you believe this request to be important for him/her/them.

My prayer for my child(ren):

_____
_____
_____
_____
_____
_____
_____
_____
_____
_____
_____
_____
_____
_____

Wednesday

How can being generous benefit your family? Take time to communicate to God why you believe this request to be important for them.

My prayer for my family:

_____
_____
_____
_____
_____
_____
_____
_____
_____
_____
_____
_____
_____

Thursday

How can being generous benefit your church and pastor? Take time to communicate to God why you believe this request to be important for them.

My prayer for my church and pastor:

_____
_____
_____
_____
_____
_____
_____
_____
_____
_____
_____
_____
_____

Friday

How can being generous benefit your boss/co-workers? Take time to communicate to God why you believe this request to be important for them.

My prayer for my boss/co-workers:

_____
_____
_____
_____
_____
_____
_____
_____
_____
_____
_____
_____
_____
_____

Saturday

How can being generous benefit your enemy? Take time to communicate to God why you believe this request to be important for them.

My prayer for my enemy/enemies:

_____
_____
_____
_____
_____
_____
_____
_____
_____
_____
_____
_____
_____
_____

Sunday

How can being generous benefit you? Take time to communicate to God why you believe this request to be important.

My prayer for myself:

_____
_____
_____
_____
_____
_____
_____
_____
_____
_____
_____
_____
_____
_____

Week 9

Matthew 6:33

*"But seek ye first the kingdom of God,
and His righteousness,
and all these things
shall be added to you."*

Explanation

The most prominent wealth is
obtained spiritually, by seeking
after the things of God.
Once you possess those,
the materialistic things will follow.

Prayer Tip

*Ask God to reveal your
spiritual voids.*

Monday

How can filling spiritual voids benefit your partner? Take time to communicate to God why you believe this request to be important for your significant other.

My prayer for my spouse (partner):

_____
_____
_____
_____
_____
_____
_____
_____
_____
_____
_____
_____
_____
_____

Tuesday

How can filling spiritual voids benefit your child(ren)? Take time to communicate to God why you believe this request to be important for him/her/them.

My prayer for my child(ren):

_____
_____
_____
_____
_____
_____
_____
_____
_____
_____
_____
_____
_____
_____

Wednesday

How can filling spiritual voids benefit your family? Take time to communicate to God why you believe this request to be important for them.

My prayer for my family:

_____
_____
_____
_____
_____
_____
_____
_____
_____
_____
_____
_____
_____

Thursday

How can filling spiritual voids benefit your church and pastor? Take time to communicate to God why you believe this request to be important for them.

My prayer for my church and pastor:

_____
_____
_____
_____
_____
_____
_____
_____
_____
_____
_____
_____
_____

Friday

How can filling spiritual voids benefit your boss/co-workers? Take time to communicate to God why you believe this request to be important for them.

My prayer for my boss/co-workers:

_____
_____
_____
_____
_____
_____
_____
_____
_____
_____
_____
_____
_____

Saturday

How can filling spiritual voids benefit your enemy? Take time to communicate to God why you believe this request to be important for them.

My prayer for my enemy/enemies:

_____
_____
_____
_____
_____
_____
_____
_____
_____
_____
_____
_____

Sunday

How can filling spiritual voids benefit you? Take time to communicate to God why you believe this request to be important.

My prayer for myself:

_____

_____

_____

_____

_____

_____

_____

_____

_____

_____

_____

_____

_____

Week 10

Luke 6:38

"Give, and it will be given to you: good measure, pressed down, shaken together, and running over. For with the same measure that you use, it will be measured to you in return."

Explanation

Whatever you give,
will be given to you.
The spirit in which you give,
will be spirit that the
gift is reciprocated.

Prayer Tip

Ask God to grant you a genuine spirit of generosity.

Monday

How can possessing a spirit of generosity benefit your partner? Take time to communicate to God why you believe this request to be important for your significant other.

My prayer for my spouse (partner):

_____
_____
_____
_____
_____
_____
_____
_____
_____
_____
_____

Tuesday

How can possessing a spirit of generosity benefit your child(ren)? Take time to communicate to God why you believe this request to be important for him/her/them.

My prayer for my child(ren):

_____
_____
_____
_____
_____
_____
_____
_____
_____
_____
_____
_____
_____

Wednesday

How can possessing a spirit of generosity benefit your family? Take time to communicate to God why you believe this request to be important for them.

My prayer for my family:

_____
_____
_____
_____
_____
_____
_____
_____
_____
_____
_____
_____

Thursday

How can possessing a spirit of generosity benefit your church and pastor? Take time to communicate to God why you believe this request to be important for them.

My prayer for my church and pastor:

_____
_____
_____
_____
_____
_____
_____
_____
_____
_____
_____
_____
_____

Friday

How can possessing a spirit of generosity benefit your boss/co-workers? Take time to communicate to God why you believe this request to be important for them.

My prayer for my boss/co-workers:

_____
_____
_____
_____
_____
_____
_____
_____
_____
_____
_____
_____
_____

Saturday

How can possessing a spirit of generosity benefit your enemy? Take time to communicate to God why you believe this request to be important for them.

My prayer for my enemy/enemies:

_____
_____
_____
_____
_____
_____
_____
_____
_____
_____
_____
_____
_____
_____

Sunday

How can possessing a spirit of generosity benefit you? Take time to communicate to God why you believe this request to be important.

My prayer for myself:

_____
_____
_____
_____
_____
_____
_____
_____
_____
_____
_____
_____
_____

Week 11

1 Corinthians 9:6

"Remember this: Whoever sows sparingly will also reap sparingly, and whoever sows generously will also reap generously."

Explanation

The spirit in which you give will directly affect the way that you receive. Always remember that you will become the recipient. Make sure that you want to receive what comes your way.

Prayer Tip

Pray that God grant you the ability to bless others.

Monday

How can blessing other people benefit your partner? Take time to communicate to God why you believe this request to be important for your significant other.

My prayer for my spouse (partner):

_____
_____
_____
_____
_____
_____
_____
_____
_____
_____
_____
_____
_____
_____

Tuesday

How can blessing other people benefit your child(ren)? Take time to communicate to God why you believe this request to be important for him/her/them.

My prayer for my child(ren):

_____
_____
_____
_____
_____
_____
_____
_____
_____
_____
_____
_____

Wednesday

How can blessing other people benefit your family? Take time to communicate to God why you believe this request to be important for them.

My prayer for my family:

_____
_____
_____
_____
_____
_____
_____
_____
_____
_____
_____

Thursday

How can blessing other people benefit your church and pastor? Take time to communicate to God why you believe this request to be important for them.

My prayer for my church and pastor:

_____
_____
_____
_____
_____
_____
_____
_____
_____
_____
_____
_____
_____

Friday

How can blessing other people benefit your boss/co-workers? Take time to communicate to God why you believe this request to be important for them.

My prayer for my boss/co-workers:

_____
_____
_____
_____
_____
_____
_____
_____
_____
_____
_____
_____

Saturday

How can blessing other people benefit your enemy? Take time to communicate to God why you believe this request to be important for them.

My prayer for my enemy/enemies:

_____
_____
_____
_____
_____
_____
_____
_____
_____
_____
_____
_____
_____

Sunday

How can blessing other people benefit you? Take time to communicate to God why you believe this request to be important.

My prayer for myself:

_____
_____
_____
_____
_____
_____
_____
_____
_____
_____
_____
_____
_____
_____

Week 12

James 4:10

*"Humble yourselves
in the sight of the Lord,
and He shall
lift you up."*

Explanation

Possessing a sense of humility is essential for kingdom work. Remember that whatever good you have done is because of God's favor. If you honor Him, He will reward you.

Prayer Tip

Pray that God always allows you to remain humble.

Monday

How can maintaining a spirit of humility benefit your partner? Take time to communicate to God why you believe this request to be important for your significant other.

My prayer for my spouse (partner):

_____
_____
_____
_____
_____
_____
_____
_____
_____
_____
_____
_____

Tuesday

How can maintaining a spirit of humility benefit your child(ren)? Take time to communicate to God why you believe this request to be important for him/her/them.

My prayer for my child(ren):

_____
_____
_____
_____
_____
_____
_____
_____
_____
_____
_____
_____
_____

Wednesday

How can maintaining a spirit of humility benefit your family? Take time to communicate to God why you believe this request to be important for them.

My prayer for my family:

_____
_____
_____
_____
_____
_____
_____
_____
_____
_____
_____
_____
_____

Thursday

How can maintaining a spirit of humility benefit your church and pastor? Take time to communicate to God why you believe this request to be important for them.

My prayer for my church and pastor:

_____
_____
_____
_____
_____
_____
_____
_____
_____
_____
_____
_____
_____

Friday

How can maintaining a spirit of humility benefit your boss/co-workers? Take time to communicate to God why you believe this request to be important for them.

My prayer for my boss/co-workers:

_____
_____
_____
_____
_____
_____
_____
_____
_____
_____
_____
_____

Saturday

How can maintaining a spirit of humility benefit your enemy? Take time to communicate to God why you believe this request to be important for them.

My prayer for my enemy/enemies:

_____
_____
_____
_____
_____
_____
_____
_____
_____
_____
_____
_____

Sunday

How can maintaining a spirit of humility benefit you? Take time to communicate to God why you believe this request to be important.

My prayer for myself:

_____
_____
_____
_____
_____
_____
_____
_____
_____
_____
_____
_____

Week 13

Psalms 118:25

*"Please, Lord,
please save us.
Please, Lord,
please give us success."*

Explanation

Whatever you achieve,
you want it to be because
God gave it to you.
It matters how you obtain
your possessions.

Prayer Tip

*Ask God to keep you honest in
all your endeavors.*

Monday

How can possessing integrity benefit your partner? Take time to communicate to God why you believe this request to be important for your significant other.

My prayer for my spouse (partner):

_____
_____
_____
_____
_____
_____
_____
_____
_____
_____
_____
_____
_____
_____

Tuesday

How can possessing integrity benefit your child(ren)? Take time to communicate to God why you believe this request to be important for him/her/them.

My prayer for my child(ren):

_____
_____
_____
_____
_____
_____
_____
_____
_____
_____
_____
_____
_____

Wednesday

How can possessing integrity benefit your family? Take time to communicate to God why you believe this request to be important for them.

My prayer for my family:

_____
_____
_____
_____
_____
_____
_____
_____
_____
_____
_____
_____
_____

Thursday

How can possessing integrity benefit your church and pastor? Take time to communicate to God why you believe this request to be important for them.

My prayer for my church and pastor:

_____
_____
_____
_____
_____
_____
_____
_____
_____
_____
_____
_____
_____

Friday

How can possessing integrity benefit your boss/co-workers? Take time to communicate to God why you believe this request to be important for them.

My prayer for my boss/co-workers:

_____
_____
_____
_____
_____
_____
_____
_____
_____
_____
_____
_____
_____

Saturday

How can possessing integrity benefit your enemy? Take time to communicate to God why you believe this request to be important for them.

My prayer for my enemy/enemies:

_____
_____
_____
_____
_____
_____
_____
_____
_____
_____
_____
_____
_____
_____

Sunday

How can possessing integrity benefit you? Take time to communicate to God why you believe this request to be important.

My prayer for myself:

_____
_____
_____
_____
_____
_____
_____
_____
_____
_____
_____
_____
_____

Epilogue

The hope is that now that you have reached the end of this journal, you have learned:

- That prayer is not just about you
- How to pray more effectively
- How to seek true prosperity

I also pray that you have become more prosperous than you were 13 weeks ago. My desire is that you have a true sense of prosperity and are not overcome with obtaining materialistic wealth. Remember to continually trust God to grant your needs and wants.

Toneal M. Jackson is a National and International Award-Winning Author; Publisher; and Inspirational Speaker. She is the founder of Artists Promoting Success, as well as #ImGladToBeAWoman, an organization that empowers women.

In 2012, CBS Chicago named her one of "5 Indie Authors and Publishers to Watch Out For". She was inducted into the Young Women's Professional League in 2016 and POWER (Professional Organization of Women of Excellence Recognized) in 2018. In 2019, she received the I Change Nations Award for her work in the literary industry. For more on Toneal, visit: www.AWEInspiringCoach.com

Other Books by Toneal M. Jackson:

Pleasing Your Partner: A Spiritual Guide to H.A.P.P.I.N.E.S.S.
Four Girls: A Lot of Choices
Four Girls Learn Their Colors
It's A Way to Say It All: How to Communicate with Your Kids
It's A Way to Say It All: How to Communicate with Your Partner
Growing Up to be Happy
She's Out. I'm In
Inspiration from A.B.O.V.E.
Learning to Love Me
Love Me...Please
Being an Authorpreneur: How to Succeed in the Book Business
The Race to the Ring: The Seven Cs of a Successful Courtship
The Fruit of the Spirit Anthology:
Taking Life's Bitter Moments and Making Them Sweet
Praying Peace Over My Life (Journal)
Praying Purpose for My Life (Journal)
Praying Problems out of My Life (Journal)
Praising through the Pandemic

www.ingramcontent.com/pod-product-compliance
Lightning Source LLC
LaVergne TN
LVHW051846080426
835512LV00018B/3089